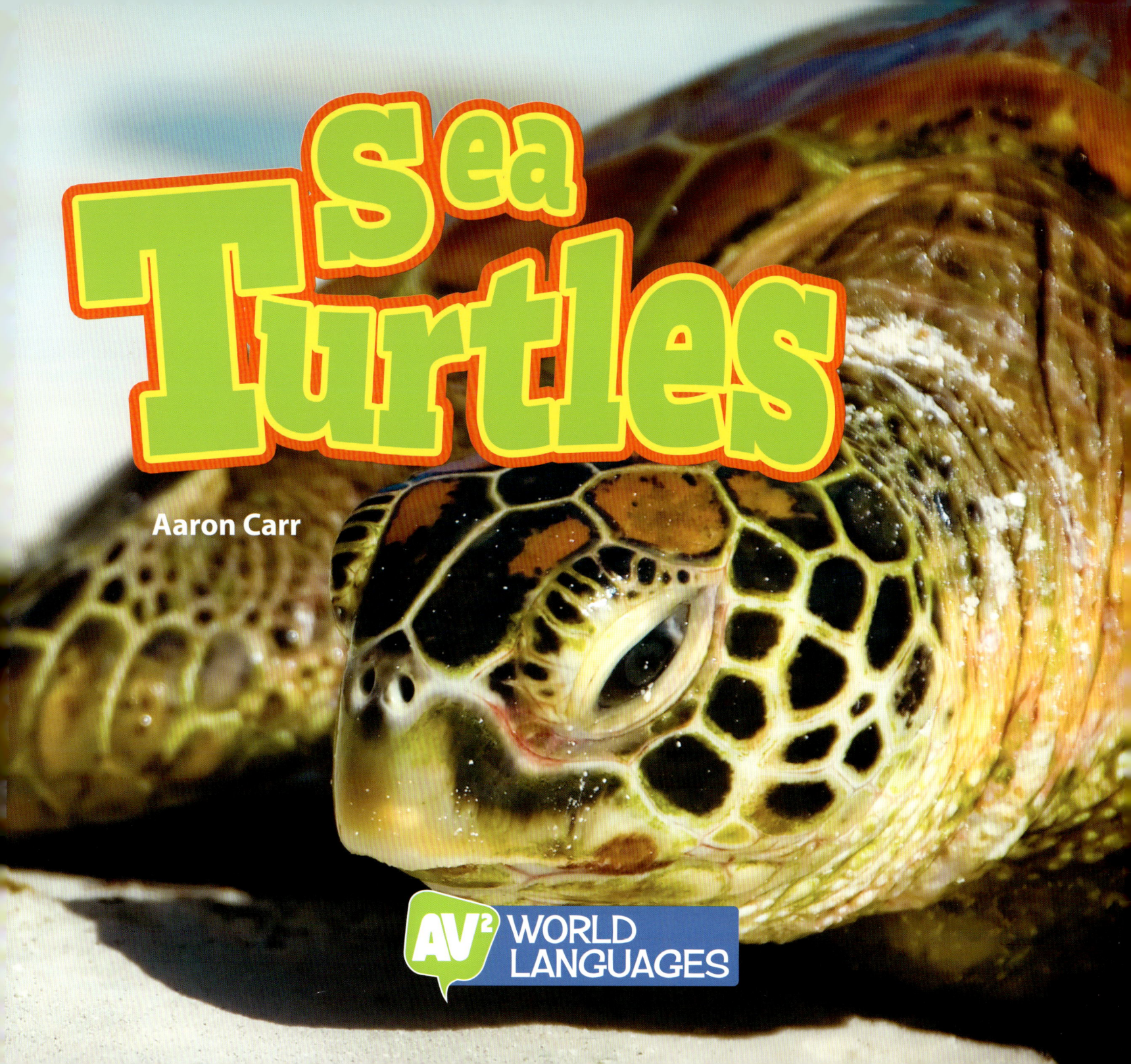
Sea Turtles

Aaron Carr

AV² WORLD LANGUAGES

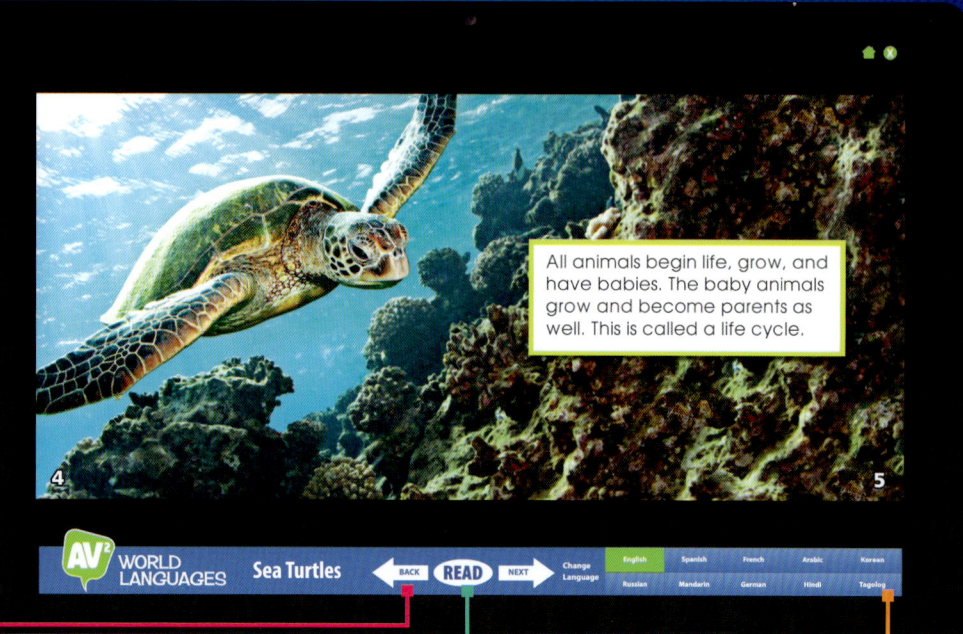

Published by AV² by Weigl
350 5th Avenue, 59th Floor New York, NY 10118
Website: www.av2books.com

Copyright ©2020 AV² by Weigl
All rights reserved. No part of this publication may be reproduced, stored in a retrieval system, or transmitted in any form
or by any means, electronic, mechanical, photocopying, recording, or otherwise, without the prior written permission of the publisher.

Library of Congress Control Number: 2019938135

ISBN 978-1-4896-7266-7 (hardcover)
ISBN 978-1-4896-7267-4 (multi-user eBook)

Printed in Guangzhou, China
1 2 3 4 5 6 7 8 9 0   23 22 21 20 19

042019
122118

Project Coordinator: Jared Siemens   Art Director: Terry Paulhus

Weigl acknowledges iStock and Getty Images as the primary image suppliers for this title.

Sea Turtles

CONTENTS

- 2   AV² Book Code
- 4   Life Cycle
- 6   Reptiles
- 8   Birth
- 10 Hatchling
- 12 Youth
- 14 Adult
- 16 Nesting
- 18 Laying Eggs
- 20 Turtles to Hatchlings
- 22 Life Cycle Quiz
- 24 Key Words

All animals begin life, grow, and have babies. The baby animals grow and become parents as well. This is called a life cycle.

6

Sea turtles are reptiles. Reptiles are cold-blooded animals. They need heat from the Sun to keep them warm.

Sea turtles are born on beaches. They hatch from eggs when they are born.

A baby sea turtle uses a bump on its nose to break out of its egg.

9

Baby sea turtles are called hatchlings. Hatchlings crawl to the ocean after they hatch.

Young sea turtles may swim thousands of miles from where they were born. They live and grow on their own for many years. People who study turtles call these the lost years.

Adult sea turtles can be more than 7 feet long when they are fully grown. They can weigh as much as a sailboat.

Sea turtles can live 80 years or more.

Adult female sea turtles leave the water to lay their eggs. This is called nesting.

Some sea turtles swim thousands of miles to nest on the beach where they were born.

A female sea turtle can lay as many as 200 eggs at one time. She hides them in the sand to keep them safe.

A sea turtle egg is about the size of a Ping-Pong ball.

There are seven kinds of sea turtles. Each kind of sea turtle may be a different size and color. A hatchling gets its size and color from its parents.

Life Cycles Quiz

Test your knowledge of sea turtle life cycles by taking this quiz. Look at these pictures. Which stage of the life cycle do you see in each picture?

Egg   Hatchling
   Youth   Adult

23

KEY WORDS

Research has shown that as much as 65 percent of all written material published in English is made up of 300 words. These 300 words cannot be taught using pictures or learned by sounding them out. They must be recognized by sight. This book contains 64 common sight words to help young readers improve their reading fluency and comprehension. This book also teaches young readers several important content words, such as proper nouns. These words are paired with pictures to aid in learning and improve understanding.

Page	Sight Words First Appearance
5	a, all, and, animals, as, grow, have, is, life, the, this, well
7	are, from, keep, need, sea, them, they, to
8	its, of, on, out, uses, when
11	after
12	call, for, live, many, may, miles, own, people, their, these, were, where, who, years, young
15	be, can, feet, long, more, much, or, than
17	leave, some, water
19	about, at, in, one, she, time
20	different, each, gets, kinds, there

Page	Content Words First Appearance
5	babies, life cycle, parents
7	heat, reptiles, sea turtles, Sun
8	beaches, eggs, nose
11	hatchlings, ocean
12	thousands
15	adult, sailboat
17	nesting
19	ball, sand, size
20	color

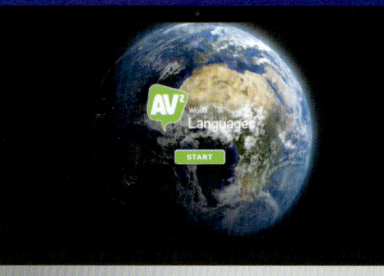

Visit **www.av2books.com** to experience your AV² World Languages title in ten languages.

Step 1 | Go to **av2books.com**

Step 2 | **Enter the code** shown here — **AVM86475**

Step 3 | **Explore** your ten eBooks and readalongs in ten languages.

www.av2books.com

24